Richard and Bridget Larn

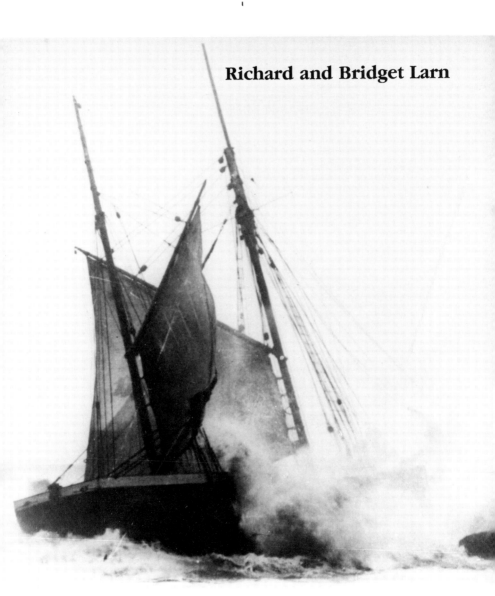

Tor Mark Press · Penryn

Other books in the series

This edition first published 1990 by Tor Mark Press,
Islington Wharf, Penryn, Cornwall TR10 8AT

© 1990 Tor Mark Press

ISBN 0-85025-324-1

Acknowledgements
The authors and publishers gratefully acknowledge the many early
photographers of shipwrecks in Cornwall, whose collections have made
this book possible, including four generations of the Gibson family,
Richard Brothers of Penzance, the Hawkes of Helston, and others. Also
the following shipwreck enthusiasts and collectors who have made
photographs available: Clive Carter, John Behenna, John Davies, John
Schofield, Peter Herbert, the Burrow and Eddyvean collections by
courtesy of the Royal Institution of Cornwall, the late Eric Collins and
others. The photographs on pages 5 and 10 are reproduced by kind
permission of St Ives Camera Company and that on page 23 by kind
permission of John Watts, Cornerways Studio, Rock.

Printed in Great Britain by The Beacon Press, Uckfield, Sussex.

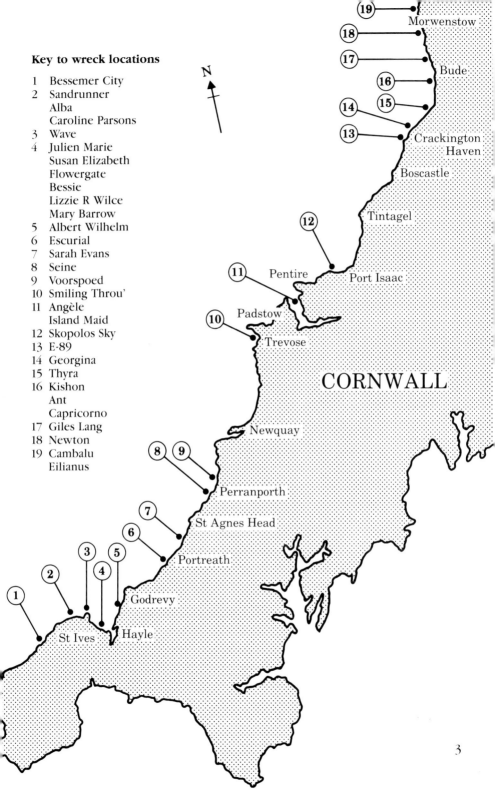

Key to wreck locations

1 Bessemer City
2 Sandrunner
  Alba
  Caroline Parsons
3 Wave
4 Julien Marie
  Susan Elizabeth
  Flowergate
  Bessie
  Lizzie R Wilce
  Mary Barrow
5 Albert Wilhelm
6 Escurial
7 Sarah Evans
8 Seine
9 Voorspoed
10 Smiling Throu'
11 Angèle
   Island Maid
12 Skopolos Sky
13 E-89
14 Georgina
15 Thyra
16 Kishon
   Ant
   Capricorno
17 Giles Lang
18 Newton
19 Cambalu
   Eilianus

N

CORNWALL

Morwenstow
Bude
Crackington Haven
Boscastle
Tintagel
Port Isaac
Pentire
Padstow
Trevose
Newquay
Perranporth
St Agnes Head
Portreath
Godrevy
Hayle
St Ives

3

Wrecked in fog to the west of Clodgy Point and St Ives on
2 November 1936, the 5686 ton American *SS Bessemer City* had
left Liverpool for London with a general cargo. She broke in two,
then went to pieces, covering beaches from Clodgy to Newquay
with cases of tinned fruit, salmon, raisins, sultanas and other
Californian produce. The wreck was relocated in 1963 when
divers recovered a quantity of zinc ingots, which led to a court
case involving theft.

The coaster *Sandrunner* found its way close inshore at
Porthmeor, St Ives, in dense fog on 31 May 1950. She was laden
with coal from Barry, for Hayle power station, and was later
successfully refloated and saved. No doubt the incident made
these children's holiday particularly memorable!

This dramatic scene on Porthmeor Beach occurred on 31 January, 1938. The 3700 ton Panamanian motor ship *Alba,* from Barry to Civitavecchia with coal, had gone ashore and the new St Ives motor lifeboat *Caroline Parsons* which went to the rescue was capsized, thrown on the rocks and damaged beyond repair. Hundreds of local people helped pull all nine lifeboatmen to safety, together with 18 of the 23 seamen saved from the *Alba.*

Opposite: The naval fleet minesweeper *Wave* was driven ashore in a north-easterly gale alongside Westcott's Quay, St Ives, where she gave the public a first class view both of a shipwreck and a classic rescue by breeches buoy. Built in 1944, the minesweeper was successfully refloated and saved; she remained in service until 1962.

The 71 ton brigantine *Julien Marie,* carrying a cargo of anthracite from Swansea to her home port Auray, failed to make St Ives harbour in a north-east gale on 5 February 1901, and was wrecked on Porthminster beach immediately beneath the railway station.

Opposite: The fifty year old collier *Susan Elizabeth,* owned by St Ives coal merchant Joshua Daniel, was caught by a north-east gale off the Mumbles near Swansea on 17 October 1907. She managed to reach St Ives, but with all but her fore topsail in ribbons she missed the entrance to the harbour and, like the *Julien Marie* opposite, was wrecked on Porthminster Beach. Captain John Curnow, previously shipwrecked on the *Jasper* at St Ives in 1874, was saved along with his crew by the local lifeboat.

Following two years service off the D-day invasion beaches as a blockship, the 5107 ton *SS Flowergate,* a requisitioned German ship, went ashore off Porthminster Beach in August 1946, whilst under tow to a breaker's yard. She was refloated to continue her final voyage.

The last coasting schooner to be wrecked at Newquay, the three-masted 54 ton *Bessie* of Truro, on passage from Cork to Penryn with a cargo of oats, dragged her anchors and went ashore under Trevelgue Head on 4 March 1912. Her crew were rescued by breeches buoy from the cliff top.

Overleaf: Porthminster Beach, scene of so many wrecks, was the site of this extraordinary double stranding on 7/8 January 1908. First the 163 ton *Lizzie R Wilce* of Falmouth, two days out from Swansea for St Malo with anthracite, missed stays, glanced off the Crab rock and drove ashore at 9pm (background); her crew were rescued by lifeboat. Eight hours later, at 5am on the 8th, the 190 ton schooner *Mary Barrow* also from Swansea with coal for the Isle of Wight stranded 200 yards away. Both vessels left Swansea within a few hours of each other and went ashore in the same place at about the same interval!

Two days out from Ramsay, Isle of Man, bound for Fowey in ballast, the 202 ton German brig *Albert Wilhelm* of Barth struck the Stones reef and drove into Lelant, near Hayle, on 16 October 1886. Five men were saved by breeches buoy and four by the Hayle lifeboat *Isis* – the last rescue of a twenty year career. As the bewildered German crew sat on the dunes watching the coastguards saving pieces of wreckage, the Glasgow steam collier *Excelsior* stranded only 65 metres from the remains of their own ship.

The best remembered shipwreck outside Portreath was the Glasgow steam collier *Escurial,* laden with 1350 tons of coal for the Adriatic port of Fiume and lost on 25 January 1895. At midnight on the 24th she had collided with a Welsh pilot cutter and started a bad leak. By 2am her boiler fires were extinguished by the rising water level. She struck the shore near Gull rock, but rocket lines fired from the shore failed to reach her; the Hayle lifeboat, brought round by road, had saved just one seaman when a wave threw her back ashore. It proved impossible to relaunch the lifeboat there, and the ship went to pieces in a matter of hours, claiming the lives of eleven crew.

Overleaf: When the wreck of the Dutch steel barquentine *Voorspoed* ebbed dry at noon on 7 March 1901, after going ashore in a gale on Perran Beach near Droskyn Point, looting started on an unprecedented scale. Captain de Grooth later stated, 'I have been wrecked in different parts of the globe even in the Fiji Islands, but never among such savages as those of Perranporth!'

The last but one sailing coaster to be wrecked near Portreath was the 55 year old 110 ton Appledore schooner *Sarah Evans*, on 27 October 1932. While carrying coal from Newport to Par, she drove under Wheal Sally cliff near Porthtowan, with most of her sails gone and her auxiliary engine not working. Captain Hopkins and his crew were rescued by the coastguards, working from the cliff top.

The French nitrate clipper ship *Seine,* of 2630 gross tons, 81 days out of Iquiquie to Falmouth 'for orders' was driven past Land's End and up the north coast of Cornwall on 28 December 1900. Early that afternoon she ran in just north of Chapel Rock and became a total wreck, but without loss of life. The wreck was sold to a Newquay captain for £42.

Visitors and locals alike went to Trevone Bay near Padstow on 20 April 1924, when the Great Yarmouth registered trawler *Smiling Throu*, built originally as the minesweeper *HMS Neaptide*, ran aground in fog. Her crew of nine saved themselves in their own boat, and the vessel was abandoned as a total loss.

As the Padstow lifeboat *Arab* lay alongside the wreck of the
Island Maid, wrecked on the dreaded Doom Bar on 13 November
1911, a schooner stormed around Stepper Point, made a violent
change of course to avoid the other two, and herself ended up on
the Bar. She was the brigantine *Angèle* of Boulogne. The lifeboat
was called out again, but failed to reach the wreck. When asked
to launch for a third time, the exhausted Padstow crew refused,
and a scratch crew was sought in Port Isaac; they reached the
vessel and saved her captain but four other crew were lost.

Broken in two, her bridge and engine room already completely underwater, the remains of the Cypriot motor vessel *Skopolos Sky* lies under the high cliffs in Hell's Mouth near Port Isaac, after going ashore on 13 March 1980.

This relic of World War Two, the captured German motor torpedo boat *E-89* broke tow on passage to a breaker's yard in Wales on 5 October 1946. She drove ashore at Crackington Haven where she went to pieces.

Carts drawn by horse were used to unload the cargo of Baltic deals from the 20 year old Glasgow barque *Georgina*, which was forced ashore by a north-westerly hurricane at Stanbury Mouth near Bude on 25 October 1865.

The *Thyra,* a Danish barquentine registered at Ronne, went ashore four miles south-west of Bude at Cleave Strand on 26 October 1896. Carrying a cargo of coal and bricks from Llanelli for Stockholm, she lost all her sails and her foremast in a gale. Her crew of nine were saved by the Bude lifeboat which, due to rough sea, could only land them at Boscastle.

After parting her tow from the tug *Australia* in bad weather, the 491 ton Shields barque *Kishon,* bound from London to Appledore for refit, drove ashore on the rocks at Bude on 7 November 1890 and became a total wreck. Her crew were saved by the rocket brigade's breeches buoy.

The fishing smack *Ant* of Bude, perched on top of the Bude breakwater after going ashore on 16 November 1868. This was the fifth time she had gone ashore locally, she was almost lost at sea off Scilly during the Great Blizzard of March 1891 and was finally sunk in a collision with the Padstow schooner *Maria* off Trevose Head in July 1897.

The 589 ton Austrian barque *Capricorno* was off Lundy Island in rough weather when she slipped her tow from the tug *Fastnet* on 27 December 1900; deep laden with coal from Cardiff destined for São Paul de Loando and unable to make any headway against the gale, she drifted to leeward and struck Bude breakwater at 1.30pm the following day. With her two lifeboats smashed to pieces, heavy seas swept her mate and seven seamen to their deaths. Although a breeches buoy was rigged between ship and shore, it became tangled. Only two crew survived, one of them by going hand over hand along the hawser of the breeches buoy, taking 45 minutes to reach safety.

Thick fog on 21 March 1886 caused the captain of the 916 ton steamship *Newton* of West Hartlepool, in ballast from Bremerhaven to Newport to load coal, to go ashore among the rocks under Higher Sharpnose. Her crew of eighteen clambered over the rocks to safety, but the vessel was broken up for scrap where she lay.

Overleaf: There are some anxious moments on 8 November 1896, when the 80 ton St Ives schooner *Giles Lang*, Porthcawl to Penzance with coal, was beached deliberately at Maer Lake after developing a serious leak. The breeches buoy was rigged successfully but then the lines fouled and it took some time to rescue the crew, spectators being called upon to assist.

Two bow sections: the 496 ton Liverpool steam coaster *Cambalu* was off course in fog – that curse of navigation before radar – when she crashed ashore below Knap Head, north of Bude, on 3 February 1933. Her crew were saved by the Padstow lifeboat, and the vessel broke up. Her gutted bow section still lay rusting on the beach when it was joined by that of another Liverpool coaster, the *Eilianus,* on 15 June 1936. Parts of both wrecks can be seen to this day amongst the rocks.